The ZOO

Written By
K.ROUSE

To grandma Florine for encouraging me to reach for the stars and show kindness to everyone.

Copyright 2021 by K A Rouse. All Rights Reserved.

No part of this book may be reproduced or transmitted in any form or by any means, electronic or mechanical, including photocopying and recording, or by any information storage and retrieval system, without permission in writing from the author and publisher.

Printed in the United States of America

2021 First Edition
10 9 8 7 6 5 4 3 2 1

Subject Index:
Rouse, K.A.

Title: Lana Banana Animal Rescuer: The Zoo

1. Children's Superhero Fiction
2. Children's Values
3. Children's Animals
4. Children's Action & Adventure
5. Titi Monkey
6. Zoo
7. Rainforest

Paperback ISBN: 979-8-9855907-0-8
Library of Congress Card Catalog Number: 2022900826

lanabananasuperhero.com

TABLE OF CONTENTS

Chapter 1: The Special Exhibit   1

Chapter 2: The Zoo   6

Chapter 3: The Rescue   16

Chapter 1

The Special Exhibit

Lana loved animals. Every time she learned about an animal, each one became her favorite. She wrote school reports on snakes, bears, dolphins, and monkeys.

It was Saturday. She was looking forward to a day out with her mom.

"Lana, we're leaving in ten minutes!" Her mom called out.

"OK. I'm trying to find my binoculars." Lana answered.

THE ZOO

Lana and her mom were going to the zoo. There was a new exhibit on the rainforest. Lana wanted to see the Spider Monkeys from South America.

She remembered visiting a similar exhibit, and many of the monkeys were hiding in the trees. Now, with her binoculars, she could get an up-close view.

THE ZOO

The ride to the zoo was only 15 minutes. Lana checked her phone for the zoo website to make sure she would recognize the Spider Monkeys. She read that this zoo had a family of ten monkeys.

"Mom, you are going to love the long arms and tails on these monkeys. Some of them have brown and black fur too!" Lana beamed.

"Really? I can't wait to see them," her mom said.

Chapter 2

The Zoo

Lana's mom pulled into the zoo's parking lot. They were lucky to find a space near the front entrance.

Lana's heart beat faster with excitement. She put her phone in her backpack and wiped the lens of her binoculars.

"OK, mom, let's go straight to the Rainforest Exhibit, " Lana said.

THE ZOO

Lana and her mom visited the zoo often. Since this was a new exhibit, Lana wanted to arrive early. She was anxious to take pictures and tell her friends about her fun day.

As soon as she entered the gate, Lana noticed the smell. It was not a bad smell. It reminded her of her grandma's greenhouse with lots of colorful flowers, plants, and vegetables.

Then she heard the sounds of falling rain and a gushing waterfall. The beautiful scene of nature felt magical.

"Mom, look over there!" Lana shouted, pointing to a macaw.

Lana went ahead of her mom. She noticed that there was a tall rope fence separating the exhibit from the public.

Lana turned back to see if her mom could keep up. That's when Lana saw the baby Spider Monkey balancing on the tree branch.

She turned and called out, "Mom, I think the baby monkey climbed out of the fence. He looks very friendly."

"Let's find the zookeeper," her mom said.

"OK," Lana replied.

The zookeeper was inside the fence with the Spider Monkeys. Lana noticed that everyone was looking up toward the sky with worried looks on their faces. The monkeys were making loud squeals and pointing towards a net on the tree.

Oh no, the baby monkey is stuck in the net. I have to save him. There's no time to waste, she thought.

Chapter 3

The Rescue

Lana ducked behind a tree. Within seconds, she appeared ready to spring into action.

For weeks, she had been practicing climbing trees with her sister. Lana was a very fast climber and was even faster coming down.

Lana told the zookeeper about the friendly Spider Monkey in the other tree. The zookeeper shook her head and smiled. She called for backup to help the other monkey.

Then Lana climbed to the top of the tree and onto the net. Everyone cheered. She crawled to the baby monkey. His long, silky tail was twisted in the rope netting. Lana gave him a banana to distract him while she carefully released his tail. The baby monkey was free!

"Thank you, Lana Banana," the zookeeper said with a smile. "You are a true animal rescuer. I must find a way to repay you for your brave act."

"That's OK. I love rescuing animals," Lana stated.

"How would you like to feed the Spider Monkeys and other animals in the rainforest?" the zookeeper asked.

Lana could not believe what she heard. "Really?" Lana replied.

"Yes, it's the least I could do for your bravery and quick thinking."

"Can I, mom?"

"Of course, you can. I'm so proud of you!" her mom beamed.

"Lana, if you don't mind, I'd like for your mom to use my camera to take a picture of you and the Spider Monkey family. I can take one with your camera as well," the zookeeper said.

"Sure!" Lana said with a bright smile. "I had no idea this trip to the zoo would turn out to be this exciting and fun."

Rainforest Facts

- Rainforests are the home to more than half of all the animals in the world.

- Rainforests cover 2% of the Earth's total surface and 6% of Earth's land surface.

- Rainforests provide air, water, food, and medicine to all plants, animals, and other living things.

- **Rainforests have four layers:**

  i) **Emergent:** the tallest trees;
  ii) **Canopy:** the leaves and branches of the trees;
  iii) **Understory:** small trees and plants; and
  iv) **Forest floor:** small plants.

Spider Monkeys

Spider monkeys look like spiders. They have long, thin arms and hook like hands to help them swing on trees. Spider monkeys do not have thumbs, yet they use their tails like hands to grab trees. These monkeys eat fruits like bananas, flowers, seeds, leaves, and small insects.

LANA BANANA Saves the Day!

Meet the Real Lana Banana

Liana Joelle attends elementary school in Southern New Jersey. Her classmates call her "Momma Liana" as she is always there to lend a hand and show kindness. At a young age, she received her first puppy, Onyx, and became a true animal lover ever since. Liana plays acoustic guitar, saxophone, and desires to be a veterinarian, engineer, and astronaut when she grows up.

About the Author

K.A. Rouse is a former corporate lawyer, business owner, author, inventor, and songwriter. She specializes in intellectual property law and has collaborated or ghostwritten over 100 books of various genres including children's, finance, inspirational, memoirs, and self-help. She is the proud mother of an adult son, two daughters, and resides in New Jersey.

Read All of The Lana Banana Series

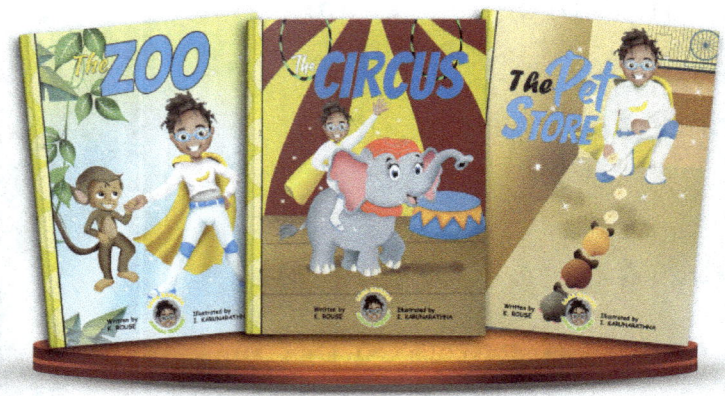

Available Now

amazon kindle | BARNES & NOBLE | nook | IngramSpark

For fun activities & more
visit: lanabananasuperhero.com

www.ingramcontent.com/pod-product-compliance
Lightning Source LLC
LaVergne TN
LVHW020416070526
838199LV00054B/3638